Consider the Gravity

Poems by

Linda Enders

Finalist in the Jonathan Holden Poetry Chapbook Contest

2023

Choeofpleirn Press

Consider the Gravity

Poems by

Linda Enders

Finalist in the Jonathan Holden Poetry Chapbook
Contest, 2023

Choeofpleirn Press

Copyright © 2023 Choeofpleirn Press

No part of this book may be reproduced, stored, or transmitted in any form, without prior permission from the author or editors. Contact choeofpleirnpress@gmail.com for permissions. Minor extracts may be quoted on social media with proper credit to the author and book title.

ISBN: (Digital) 979-8-9885631-1-2
       (Print) 979-8-9885631-2-9

Cover painting by Bernd Enders

Also available from Choeofpleirn Press
Vivienne Shalom's *The Truth Is*
     (Winner of the JH Poetry Chapbook Contest, 2023)
Amy Schumer's *Orbital Debris*
     (Winner of JH Poetry Chapbook Award, 2022)
Fran Schumer's *Weight*
     (Finalist of JH Poetry Chapbook Contest, 2022)

Choeofpleirn Press
Leavenworth, KS 66048
choeofpleirnpress@gmail.com
www.choeofpleirnpress.com

Dedication

For Eunice and Earl

Table of Contents

Rising Tide

Suddenly, after decades of silence,
the sound of surf fills the house.

The gilt-framed seascape on the wall
spills saltwater onto the polished parquet.

A seagull shrieks out of the mirror,
circles the crystal chandelier & disappears.

A stiff wind blows the door off its hinges,
and sand piles up against the furniture.

The kitchen timer won't stop announcing:
What's done is done! What's done is done!

The rising tide swirls around your feet.
Seaweed tangles around your ankles.

You slosh down the long hall.
Murky water splashes up around your knees.

At the top of the stairs, you slam the door
against the lap-lap-lap of the waves.

You pull a comforter close around you,
open a window, lean out into the dark.

The lighthouse flashes; its beam reaches out
over a vast, gray, empty expanse of sea.

Come Close

Follow the bee's hum
to the blossom too tiny to see.

Follow the tree trunk's whitewash
up to the barn owl's branch.

Follow the whiff of smoke
back to a town that was—

It only takes a spark and
a whole neighborhood's gone.

The ash that coats your car
was a bunkbed and a ball.

Although it means nothing
against what's to come,

You sweep dry leaves & pine needles
away from the door.

Everything in the world comes closer,
the poet wrote—even God, even death

No Safe Harbor

The sun pours down like honey
on the children in the morning
whose bodies wash up at midnight
upon the islands' beaches,

Who sailed out into darkness
to escape death on the doorstep
of the one & only home they'll ever know.

They are leaning out for love.
They will lean that way forever,

for their boat is lost and sinking
far from the harbor of tomorrow

which is trouble, which is hunger,
which is suffering, a death no better
than this drowning in the ocean
that embraces with a lap and
rocks them gently in her waves.

Get the Picture

A couple thousand puzzle pieces spill onto the table. You need patience, good light, clear vision, and you must concentrate. Tens of thousands die, one by one, while you shelter safe at home. There's no baseball on the radio. Shut the door, sit down and begin. Feel through the odd shapes, one by one, to find edges that fit together to form a frame. Study the picture on the box; it is your roadmap—can you find the road? There is no road. Children are hungry. Everyone is afraid. Tens of thousands are dying, one by one.

Pandemic Spring Morning

I don't see the usual pair of flickers outside the
      kitchen window the morning
the egret sweeps down on magnificent white
      wings, settles her shining feathers

into a slender profile of danger, picks her spindly
      black-legged way
among rosebushes and snaps up several
      unsuspecting lizards for lunch.

So far, in this valley of the shadow of death, I am
      on the inside looking out.
I have everything I need, want for nothing—and
      yet, I am afraid.

A musician gone here, a poet there, an actor, a
      scientist, a police officer,
a mother dies alone, a father, brother, sister,
      daughter, son—gone.

For a time, the tall white bird stands on one leg as
      if to pose for the media.
Then—as suddenly as she appeared—she, too, is
      gone.

Reasons to Welcome Autumn 2020 to California in Spite of Politics & the Pandemic

Because a fiery summer, full of chaos and fury, has come
    to an end.

Because it's not yet winter.

Because of deep purple, dark red, every shade of orange
    and tawny gold.

Because the leaves transform from glory to glory, and the
    trees let them go.

Because, like the trees, you have much to let go.

Because you can count on the neighbor to complain
    again that autumn blows
all the leaves from the liquid amber trees up and down
    our street into *her* yard.

Because of blackberries, pears, pomegranates, pumpkins
    and steamy mugs of tea.

Because it's Halloween, and the mask and the macabre
    are welcomed by all.

Because it's a sombre season populated by super heroes,
    skeletons and ghosts.

Because the time has come to light candles against the
    gathering dark.

What Are We Humans But a Brief Elaboration of a Tube

Picture a tube through which the wind blows and
        the water flows.
You squeeze in, stretch out in all directions.

Life is not a path, not a journey.

Who knows where the wind blows, where
        the water flows?
You squeeze in, stretch out in all directions.

Animal, vegetable or mineral? a voice asks.

Who knows where the wind blows, where
        the water flows?

Notes of music flow from a silver flute.
The wind whistles across the prairie all the way
        to the sea.

Animal, vegetable of mineral? a voice asks.
You diminish, disappear, stretch out into eternity.

Life is not a path, not a journey.

The wind whistles across the prairie all the way
        to the sea.
You picture a tube through which the wind blows and
        the water flows.

Mother

When Mother dies, you know
what has always been so.
Where Mother goes, you go.

Insider her body, she allows
your body to grow, shares
her being, so you can be.

Her labor propels you
from that small space
into a larger place.

Her body nourishes yours,
then weans you away
in that one way.

You obey her rules
sometimes, or not.
You love her, honor her,
or not.

But when Mother dies, you know.
You know what has always been so.
Where Mother goes, you go.

How to Draw a Redwood

To scale—not in board feet.
From a humble perspective.

Take the line up as high as you can reach,
and out as wide as your wingspan.

Focus on a tiny cone, a patch of reddish bark,
the green tip of a branch.

Listen for the heartbeat deep within,
deep down, spread out and reaching up.

In the redwood tree's height and width
there's all the time in the world.

Consider the Gravity

Consider the gravity of the rose petal
when it falls onto the table
just as he tosses aside his tie
and her skirt drops to the floor.

Turbulence in the atmosphere
creates a twinkle in the eye that,
according to our fathers and mothers,
became you and I.

When Women Were Birds

When women were birds,
some were hawks, some were doves.

When women were rattlesnakes,
they learned to silence the rattle,
to go for the surprise attack.
They learned to catch the world off guard,
no one knowing what to expect until, at last,
it became unnecessary to strike at all,
a certain balance was achieved,
a kind of peace among men.

When women were birds,
some were hawks, some were doves.

Highway Robbery

I want that little barn.
I want the three-legged stool.
I want Grandpa balanced there,
his head leaned against the cow.

I want that place.
I want that summer.
I want that time before
the Interstate was even an idea,
before the fight that broke his heart,
before the bulldozers.

I want that garden.
I want Grandma, kneeling
between rows
in the strawberry patch,
her fingers feeling
for the perfect ripeness.

I want that grapevine
with its purple bunches
next to the gravel drive
where my pal and I would ride
our imaginary horses,
Cowboys and Indians,
Lone Ranger & Tonto.

And now, strangely enough,
I want that thief of a highway,
that line on the map that connects
here to there, then to now.
I want the road that carried my
love and me in his red El Camino,
Hi-yo Silver! and away.

Turn the Wheel Into a Skid

Whatever happened to the dad I used to have,
who never embarrassed me with wild applause,
never signed the back of a report card,
never read what the teacher wrote inside?

Dinners grew cold while he finished a cigarette.
When it was time to go to church,
he was nowhere to be found.

He preferred a dim tavern at the edge of town
to the fluorescent lights at the Assemblies of God,
the company of a bartender to that of my sisters and me
or even our mother, who allowed no liquor in the
house—
except what was on his breath—who liked to say,
Your father loves you in his own way.

You talk too much, he told me. *Do as I say, not as I do.*
What little advice he gave me was good:
Look both ways, even when the light is green,
Turn the wheel into a skid.

I wonder what happened to the list of things
I needed my father to be, who could never be
more or less than the man he was, not even
so much as a disappointment now.

Collection

There was a time when you would try
to make something of this pile of rocks,

perhaps some sort of balancing act
or the outline of a path among the marigolds.

But today, you stand by the road
to offer them, one by one, to passersby.

As each stone passes from hand to hand,
you feel lighter.

Any day now, you'll be ready
to let yourself go.

The Soul Again

Odd, isn't it, that the soul wants to go on and on.
The body says: *wait, slow down, stop awhile.*

But the soul runs on ahead, dances up the path,
flies up into the clouds, slides down the waterfall

into the quiet pool, frolics and climbs out
to do it all—over and over again.

The soul will not be contained in a frail body.
This is where the idea of eternal life comes from.

The body fortifies itself to avoid the final call.
The soul listens for the bell to ring.

When the Time Comes

When the time comes
for one last ride,
I will go with you to the river.

We will go by horse-drawn carriage.
Wear whatever you like—
the new shoes, perhaps a hat.

We'll take a picnic—
the bread and the wine, of course.
Some cheese, chocolate, a few strawberries.

We'll spread a blanket
on the grassy bank
where the river is wide.

From there we will watch as
the ferry begins the journey
from the other side.

Ursula

Slow and steady she rows
across the wide sea of old age,
in and out of ports
until she grows tired of rowing,
loses interest in harbors,
sets herself adrift.

I could scarcely find her,
even with a spyglass.

At last she floats away,
all the way away,
over the horizon, gone.

Grief confounds relief.
I loosen my grip on the oars,
let the spyglass drop.

Lap of waves the only sound,
my boat begins a sideways drift.
I take hold of the oars and
row, steady and slow.

Practice Your Escape

When you hear the music playing as
the midnight show is ending,
when you feel the trade winds warm and
blowing, softly blowing,
then practice your escape.

When you breathe the heady fragrance
of the springtime madly blooming,
when your hips take you swaying
out into the early morning where
the mocking bird is mocking and
the crow is cawing, cawing.

Before you do the math and
before your bag is packed,
you must practice your escape.

By elephant or airplane,
by moped or Ferrari,
by soaring kite or camel,
you are going, surely going.

I Wish in the Humdrum of Your Heart

I wish in the humdrum of your heart
you would let me be the window
you climb through when you must
escape a world gone mad.

I imagine the ladder as it drops
down to the alley, and your feet,
too long confined inside sensible shoes,
begin to dance down the street.

Never Seen a Sky in My Life Happier
than the Sky Today

After the thin gray clouds of morning blew away
to pile up against the Sierra Nevada mountains
         in the east,
the big tropical clouds began chasing each other
         in from the west,
all the way from Honolulu, bumping up against
         each other
like wedding reception balloons—

big white puffs sashaying in, blowing by way up high,
blowing by slow, bringing a palm-tree-white-sand
         feeling,
a feeling that make us sway our hula hips
as the blue of the sky dances with the white of the clouds
that might bring a rain shower here or there, but really,
nothing so serious, maybe a mist out of the blue
or a rainbow against the faraway hill...

it's a happy sky dance between the blue and the white,
not a waltz or a two-step, just a to-and-fro or a do-si do
no threat, no thrill but a feeling of aloha, a feeling of just
         plain
happiness falling all around on the flowers and the trees
         and me.

Free Day at the Museum

--after Johnny Cash

I been everywhere, man
up and down the stairs, man
elevators, corridors and galleries, man
shops, cafes and plazas, man
through every door, across every floor
I been everywhere.

Restrooms, water fountains and trash cans, man
the whole place a rolling party, man
multi-racial and generational
I been everywhere.

Paintings, pottery and sculpture, man
poodle skirts, pony tails, ten-gallon hats
video projections as tall as the wall
a boulder way up in the air—can you dig it
I been everywhere.

No Frida but lots of Diego, man
No Cassatts—so many Monets
Jackson Pollack but no O'Keeffe
Picasso Picasso Picasso, man
I been almost everywhere.

The Lucky Stars play country
the boppers strut and spin
palm trees, temps at ninety degrees
acres and acres of cars, man
Hollywood mansions and traffic jams
I been everywhere.

21

July

Mornings, Lizard stalks bugs
for breakfast on the patio,
motionless on warm concrete
until—gobble—and he's gone.

In the afternoon, Lizard naps,
drapes his black length
over a rock on the garden wall,
blinks but does not move.

In the evening, Lizard sprints
start-stop-start alongside me,
does ten push-ups for fun,
disappears between stones.

Will Owl see him, I wonder,
when Lizard comes out
in the moonlight
to stare at the stars?

Autumn Shimmer

Early morning in autumn
when I open my window to the world,
the soft yellow of sunrise
washes over the hillside.

Pyracantha branches reach
out from the brambles and
red berries begin to glow
as if lit from within.

Early morning in autumn
when I open my window to the world,
hummingbird flashes her colors,
loops away into the mellow orange
of morning light—

Where is sorrow now?

Disassemble

You took a bicycle
by the handlebars
and twisted it
into the head of a bull.

Pablo Picasso, you
had many muses.
Their names were
Olga, Ferdinande, Dora,
Marie-Therese and Jacqueline.

With Olga you danced
and danced, but
Olga's conventional stage
was much too small. You
whirled away with Ferdinande.

The other muses you lit into,
tore apart and put together
until one began to resemble
the next and then each
disappeared altogether.

Some, like Humpty Dumpty,
could not put themselves
back together again.
Two came completely undone,
one by the rope, another by the gun.

Now, Pablo Picasso, I
make you my muse,
I disassemble you
according to my will.
I dance away. Whole.

Anna Mathilda McNeil Whistler

Unwilling to bow
to the fashion of the day,
but dressed all in gray,
white lace at the collar,
she agreed to sit for him.

If you require this task of me,
she said to son James,
you will allow me to sit up erect
and look straight ahead while
you fuss with your colors and brushes.

And if you cannot abide my direct gaze
for those many long hours, then
I shall turn my whole body to the side,
and I shall think my own thoughts.

Ode to Adam Steltzner, NASA Chief Engineer, Creator of the Sky Crane that Lowered the Curiosity & Perseverance Rovers onto the Surface of Mars

You *send* me, Adam Steltzner—

That's what my mother would say
about this feeling I have for you—

You *send* me, honest you do.

It would be true to say,
I love you like a proud mother,
and it would also be true to say
I love you like I love George Clooney,
over the moon…swoon…

In high school, they say,
you were all about rock and roll
and being cool—not books,
but music consumed you.

Won't add up to much, your dad said—
junior college will have to do.

But the movement of constellations
captured your imagination,
made you curious—

Look here, your astronomy teacher said,
standing back from the telescope.

What you saw out there

rocked your world.

What *you* say is that your Curiosity's
landed on Mars—and now your Perseverance
roves around Mars, too.

You thrill me, Adam Steltzner,
oh, yes—it's true.

Leonard

The one who knew the secret chord,
The one that pleased the Lord--
Leonard Cohen is dead.

You want it darker, he said.
He who understood so much
misunderstood our grammar.

Leonard Cohen is dead, and
these blue notes I carry around
in my pocket are not the hymns
I memorized when I was a child.

I left the binoculars on a hotel balcony.
I cannot search the heavens for Leonard
or for the great horned owl,
whose call is a question.

I wait for an answer to arrive on the wind.
A jet plane screams across the sky.
Purple was dark enough for me.

Leonard Cohen is dead.
The one who knew the secret chord,
The one who pleased the Lord.

Hallelujah.

Tony

--for Margie Heckelman

Out of the range of any lens,
his tormented soul flies free.
Frail moth finally tired
of throwing himself
against unyielding glass.
Anthony Bourdain, consumed
by the flame of international fame.

His body took its fill of life and more. Too much
through the eyes for the brain to process. Too much
through the mouth for the belly to stomach. Too much
of the loud music of longing, of unrequited hunger.

His heart shattered
with the effort
to contain so much love.
Only God's hands
are big enough
to hold the whole world.

The adrenaline forced
through the rivers of his body
broke through every dam,
flooded the banks of reason,
and in one last,
brilliant burst of light,
he was gone.

Dear Louise Gluck,

I want to speak to you in private.

I want to speak to you
as a penitent speaks
to a priest in confession.

I want to speak to you
as a patient on the couch
to her analyst.

I want to speak to you
of what is essential and
not with words alone

but through my tone
and my cadence and (what you call)
ringing imperatives.

There are poems that seem
to speak only and especially
to me.

Something rises up
a strong desire
that answers back

yes yes yes

Acknowledgments

Sincere gratitude to the editors who have published my work and given it a life in the world:

Marin Poetry Center Anthology 2014, Peg Alford Pursell, Editor, "Ursula"

Marin Poetry Center Anthology 2015, Alyse Rall Benjamin & Deborah Fass, editors,
"Highway Robbery"

Marin Poetry Center Anthology 2016, Catlyn Fendler, Editor, "The Soul Again"

"Pandemic Puzzle Poems," selected by Diane Frank and Prartho Sereno, Blue Light Press, 2021. "Get the Picture," "Pandemic Spring Morning," "Reasons to Welcome Autumn 2022 to California in Spite of Politics and the Pandemic"

Marin Poetry Center Anthology 2022, Sian Killingsworth, Editor, "Rising Tide"

Changing Harm to Harmony, Bullies & Bystanders Project, Joe Zaccardi, Editor, "Disassemble"

This, Too, Was a Gift, Ghost Ranch Fall Writing Festival Anthology, 2018, "Collection"

Many of the poems in this collection first appeared in anthologies created by classmates in the ongoing class, "The Poetic Pilgrimage, Writing Poetry as Spiritual Practice" at the College of Marin in Kentfield, CA. I owe endless gratitude to all of them—especially to our teacher, esteemed poet, Prartho Sereno.

Notes

The underlying rhythm for "No Safe Harbor" comes from the Leonard Cohen song, "Suzanne."

The phrase "A brief elaboration of a tube" comes from the Leonard Cohen song, "Going Home."

The title for the poem "When Women Were Birds" was inspired by the book of the same title written by Terry Tempest Williams.

"Tony" was written for my friend, Margie Heckleman, who grieved with me the death by suicide of the inimitable Anthony Bourdain.

"You Send Me" is a line from the song, "You Send Me," by Sam Cooke.

The repeated phrase "I been everywhere, man" in "Free Day at the Museum" is reminiscent of the song "I've Been Everywhere," written by Geoff Mack in 1959, and made popular by Johnny Cash and many others.

Judge's Comments

Linda Enders has given us a collection of poems for the trying times we live in. While these poems address issues such as climate change, migrants seeking new homes and lives, the losses and grief of death, they also allow us to share in joyful memories, take a quirky look at the paintings of Picasso and James McNeil Whistler, hear the "Hallelujah" of Leonard Cohen, and eavesdrop on the poet's request to speak to Louise Gluck in private. This collection is delightful and poignant, insightful, and inviting. Many of the poems are short, tight, and pack a punch, concluding with lines like "In the redwood's height and width/there's all the time in the world" and "The body fortifies itself to avoid the final call./The soul listens for the bell to ring." Reading this collection is very much like the final stanza of "Autumn Shimmer": "Early morning in autumn/when I open my window to the world,/ the hummingbird flashes her colors,/loops away into the mellow orange/of morning light--/Where is sorrow now?" This is the question many of these poems ask, addressing the contradiction and complication of our existence.

Anita Skeen, 2023 Judge
Author of *Never the Whole Story*;
The Resurrection of the Animals;
Outside the Fold, Outside the Frame;
and *Each Hand a Map*

Joseph Zaccardi's Comments
About the Book

Linda Enders' brilliance, in *Consider the Gravity*, is in the way she weaves the elements of the natural and human worlds. Her observations and articulations are breathtaking, taking in so much, giving so much; illuminating the dark, traversing the physical, the material, and the symbolic.

Enders inhabits the spirit and gravity of poetry while bringing her individual voice to her poems. To wit: The body fortifies itself to avoid the final call.

Joseph Zaccardi, Poet Laureate of
Marin County, California, 2013 -2015

About the Poet

Linda Enders fell in love with poetry in high school, but she did not seriously engage with writing poetry until after her retirement more than a decade ago. At that time, she enrolled in a community college class that continues to study many poets and to share one another's poems. Linda also participates in poetry retreats at a retreat center not far from her home and is a member of the Marin Poetry Center. She and her artist husband live next to open space, enjoy the company of lizards, coyote, and quail. Their home is filled with books, music and art.

Jonathan Holden Poetry Chapbook Contest

2023 Winner and Finalist

Choeofpleirn Press

Jonathan Holden Poetry Chapbook Contest
Sponsored by Choeofpleirn Press

Poets without a published chapbook or poetry book may enter.

Contest Fee: $20

Prize: 10 copies of printed chapbook and $250

See Submission Guidelines at

www.choeofpleirnpress.com/poetry-chapbook-contest

for details.

Choeofpleirn Press
www.choeofpleirnpress.com
choeofpleirnpress@gmail.com